Mountain Biking

In the High Country of Steamboat Springs, Colorado

By

Thomas R. Litteral

AMERICAN KESTREL PRESS
Steamboat Springs, Colorado

Printed in United States of America

First Edition

ISBN 1-883966-00-0 : $10.95

Front and Rear cover designs in part by Steamboat Design Associates

Cover photograph: The Author on Walton Peak, near Steamboat Springs, Colorado

All photography by the Author.

CONTENTS

PREFACE

Mountain biking is an activity that has some risks and dangers when riding in the High Country. Conditions may change rapidly in the Rocky Mountains. The climatic factors, trail conditions, and other trail users can affect each outing differently. There are both natural and man–made obstacles, long distances, and climatic forces to overcome while riding.

Some areas may be closed to mountain bike riding such as Wilderness Zones or Study areas, environmentally sensitive areas, or private property. Every attempt has been made to be sure the trails listed are open and available. The author has ridden each of the trails in this guide and is reasonably sure of their accuracy as portrayed in the descriptions and maps.

The Author and Publisher assume no responsibility for those using this guide and may not be held liable in any manner, for any inconveniences or damages that result from such usage.

ACKNOWLEDGEMENTS

It has been a great privilege to gain the assistance of the dedicated staff of various offices in Routt County, the City of Steamboat Springs, and Routt National Forest. In particular, I wish to thank a few individuals and Departments for their time and expertise in answering questions, finding proper names for trails, and route planning.

The Routt County Search and Rescue gave information about back country preparedness and mishaps. The Routt County Riders are thanked for their interest in this project and their input to the National Forest Service on conditions of current trails. Lisa Fleming of Steamboat Design Associates provided assistance in cover designing.

Chris Wilson of the City of Steamboat Springs Parks and Recreation Department; the Stagecoach State Recreation Area staff; Rob Schmitzer, Steve Hoots, and Jeff Guildehaus (former Trails specialist) at Hahn's Peak Ranger District of Routt National Forest all assisted with trail locations and conditions; and a special thank you to all the trail crews of the Routt National Forest who work the long tiring hours to create and maintain the mountain bike trail system.

FORWARD

Wwhat a wonderful place to ride a bicycle! Steamboat Springs is nestled in the Yampa Valley on the west slope of the Rocky Mountains. It is surrounded on three sides by forested mountains with two Wilderness Areas within sight of downtown. There is a world class ski resort and a first rate city owned ski and recreation complex right in town. It is an active city and its citizens take pride in the community.

The City of Steamboat Springs is committed to quality recreation. It is finishing a "crown jewel" for bicyclists, a million dollar pathway along the Yampa River which flows through the heart of town. This wide pathway is nearly 5 miles long and is a perfect place for bikers, walkers, or in-line skaters. This kind of commitment to recreation and quality of life for the residents and visitors speaks very highly for the community.

There is a network of trails throughout Steamboat Springs mostly on designated paths off the streets and sidewalks. The community continues to devote resources to planning and improving facilities available to its mountain biking residents and visitors.

The United States Forest Service has continued to recognize its role in outdoor recreation in the Routt National Forest that surrounds Steamboat Springs. There is an ever increasing demand on the resources available to recreationists. Mountain bikers have been well represented in the planning process for managing the National Forest.

There is a continuing interest locally to create, improve, and guide mountain bike trail use. This is of tremendous importance. It can really make a difference to get involved in recreation planning or to give the local planners the feedback necessary to make informed decisions.

You will find that there are nearly unlimited opportunities to ride and explore the mountains and valleys of the Steamboat Springs area. I hope that you will get out and take advantage of those opportunities and make your biking season a safe and enjoyable one.

The Rabbit Ears Peaks are familiar landmarks for all travelers over the Continental Divide near Steamboat Springs. The stone monument marks a good starting point for riding into the High Country along the Continental Divide. This trailhead is just east of the Dumont Lake Campground on old US 40. (The Rabbit Ears Peaks are in the upper right).

SINGLE TRACK VS. 2-TRACK

A single track trail is just that...a single lane treadway. Some will be as easy as this section of the Midway Trail but others are quite difficult.

A typical US Forest Service 2-track. Most are open to motor vehicles but usually receives little traffic. This two-track (FR 471A) is off the Greenville Loop along Big Creek near Clark.

INTRODUCTION

WELCOME TO THE HIGH COUNTRY OF STEAMBOAT SPRINGS, COLORADO

This guide is designed to assist the mountain bike rider in finding the right path to ride while bicycling in the area of Steamboat Springs in Colorado. Many vacationers and those new to the area are faced with the task of finding the right place to take their mountain bikes when they arrive in town. There are many wonderful options available, many scenic places to ride, and many challenging trails to test one's skills and endurance. The rides outlined in this guide are rated by means of a combination of challenges, preparation required, and the route of the trail itself.

That brings us to the purpose of this guide. Where to get out and ride. That is, where to ride within your personal ability in the current conditions. A bicycle is only a mechanical device used to convey the rider to places new and delightful. It is also a means to a terrific aerobic work-out that may test one's physical preparation. In the mountains of the Steamboat Springs area both rides can be had at once!

Steamboat Springs is located well above a mile high in elevation at 6700 feet above sea level. That factor alone can fatigue a "flat-lander" in the first few miles of a ride. A ride in the nearby mountains at 10,000 feet of altitude with its reduced oxygen available can make a seemingly simple ride into quite a challenge.

There are several factors to be aware of when you are going to take to the trails. The weather, the difficulty of the terrain, the altitude, and most important of all, your own personal fitness level and current ability. It may take a few hours to a few days to adjust to the change of altitude if you are arriving from somewhere lower in elevation. A "reduced" first outing will give you a good feel as to how ready you are for the challenging rides of the high country.

I strongly urge newly arriving riders to become acclimated to the altitude before venturing out into the National Forests or high country trails. This can be accomplished with some time, easy rides, and preplanning any trips. I cannot stress it enough that it will take you longer to ride "at altitude" with the thinner air and demanding terrain.

If you are especially interested in biking the tougher trails of the high country right away, I also recommend a test ride for yourself or your party. Find out what level of fitness and readiness you are for Steamboat Springs mountain biking. A suggested route for this test ride is to start on the west end of the Yampa Core Trail within the city limits of Steamboat Springs. Follow the paved road (20 Mile Road) to the south until it turns to gravel about seven miles out of town.

By picking this simple route that has a gentle uphill grade, you will quickly get a clue to your own personal fitness level. In the short time it will take you to peddle the 14 mile round trip you will experience the feel of what it is like to bicycle at the "lower" elevation of Steamboat Springs.

A shorter but more vigorous test ride is to Fish Creek Falls, a popular tourist attraction just east of town. That route starts at the main post office following Fish Creek Falls Road. It is much steeper but only 4 miles to the base of the falls from downtown Steamboat Springs. The first 2 miles of this route are paved then the road turns to hard packed gravel to the parking lot at the falls.

If you found the grade on either ride too much to complete or you found yourself "gasping for air like a guppy out of water" then the toughest high country trails may not be for you. If you found that the trip took a bit of effort but you could still maintain a pace all the way and carry on a conversation with your riding partners, then proceed with caution on your well planned trips to the mountains. If the route is a sheer breeze with little extra effort, then enjoy all the routes and challenges that Steamboat Springs area biking has to offer.

Being in control of your bike is the best preventative to accidents and close encounters with other trail users. Practice bike handling skills before tackling the hardest trails. Remember, horses and hikers have a right to be on the trails too (in most cases) and it is the responsibility of bikers to yield right of way to *all* others on the trail.

Riding responsibly is just that, be aware of where you are riding (do you need permission?) and are you having an undue impact upon the trail? Many trails in this guide have sections that travel through private land. Please respect the rights of the land owners and remain on the trails in those areas. As a reminder, designated Wilderness Areas are totally out of bounds for mountain bikes.

When trails or roads are soft, mountain bikes can do considerable damage to the pathway. Wait until the season is correct for high country travel or until conditions are acceptable for bikes. The National Forest Service office can assist in advising which trails are currently open and available in their areas.

I would recommend that you become acquainted with your equipment so that you can repair the minor problems such as flat tires, slipped chains, or cables that come loose. Take along the necessary tools to accomplish those repairs and know how to use them. The extra weight is very insignificant when faced with the alternative of walking back to the starting point after a breakdown. A walk out often will mean up to 5 times the amount of time it took to bicycle out there!

This also brings up the very serious topic of personal safety while biking in the backcountry. There is a very talented group of people involved in the Search and Rescue teams of the area. They respond to many bicyclist mishaps in the backcountry. Many of the accidents have occurred where riders were not using their best judgment, made a mistake in route planning, or riding beyond their ability. Whatever the real cause, it is rarely a mechanical failure. Most accidents are due to human error, not the mountain bike's fault.

Here are a few suggestions to make your trip into the backcountry safer and more enjoyable. The first suggestion is to plan your trip. Make sure you have sufficient information to find your path and have allowed the time to follow it. Take along a map of the route, use a compass at the start and midpoint to orient yourself as to where you are along the trip. Don't rely on a compass only after you are lost. Knowledge is the key to finding your way.

A second suggestion is to ride within your capabilities. A thrilling descent can turn sour very quickly if you forget to use your front and rear brakes properly. It is very necessary to have complete control over your bike at all times. If a section is too tough for your ability to safely ride through..don't ride it. Know when its time to walk that bike the short distance that it usually takes to safely pass the obstacles or hazardous parts of a pathway.

Be in sufficient physical shape to accomplish the ride you have planned. The distances seem to lengthen at altitude. There is roughly one-half the oxygen available at 10,000 feet than at sea level. This factor alone makes it much more difficult to ride long distances in the high country without excess fatigue.

A third suggestion is to take along a self-rescue kit when biking in the backcountry. Every time you leave "civilization" you may not be found for hours or days if you have a problem. A self-rescue kit should cover the bare necessities if you find yourself unable to complete your trip. A simple kit should consist of items like a first-aid kit, a couple of foil blankets (pocket sized), waterproofed matches, a meal bar (such as a PowerBar®), and a plastic whistle for signaling.

A completed knapsack or fanny pack of these items should be prepared beforehand for use each time you venture out into the wilds. This self-rescue kit will be covered in more detail in a later chapter.

A final thought, if you have not left an itinerary with a third party, who will know where you might be if you are unable to get out?. This is especially important for solo riders.

Mountain biking in the Steamboat Springs area is truly an enjoyable experience with some of the most scenic trails available in Colorado. With the help of this guide, you will be more prepared to have a safe and rewarding experience biking in the High Country of Steamboat Springs, Colorado.

A great view toward California Park from the first saddle of the Nipple Peak Trail (longer option). It takes good gearing and strong legs to climb without excess fatigue. The long loop trail around Nipple Peak with its rewarding views is for advanced riders only.

GEARING AND EQUIPMENT

Mountain bikes can be set up to ride the most rigorous routes with shock absorbing systems, cushion seats, and light alloy frames and parts. Mountain bikes are stronger, more durable, and designed specifically for high torque output. Road bikes and most hybrid bicycles are not sufficiently built to withstand the rigors of backcountry travels. At this time, fat tires, strong short frames, and 26" wheels are the best combination available for safe and comfortable bicycle travel off road.

The routes in the mountains can vary from easy gravel roads, 2-track jeep trails, or to the classical single tracks of the high country. The type of mountain bike chosen, and how it is equipped is a large factor in deciding on where you can ride.

Get a quality bike from a reputable dealer. They will usually guide your choice of bikes to the style and ability of the rider. A reputable dealer will also stand behind their sales. They want satisfied customers not just volume sales. Dealers are also a wealth of information about bicycling techniques and specialized equipment.

Mountain bikes can also be rented. That is an excellent way to find out if the type of bike fits your style and that High Country biking is really for you. Many shops will allow a "try before you buy" policy for serious mountain bikers. Renting a comparable bike to the one you might purchase will give you a realistic base to judge for yourself what kind of bike is for you.

Riding in the High Country requires some special attention to the mechanics of your bicycle. That doesn't necessarily mean a major expense or major alteration of the

1

shiny new bike you bought. What it does mean is that it's much better being prepared for the steeper climbs and sharper descents of off-road riding. The altitude and general ruggedness of the terrain place special demands on mountain bikes and their riders.

Before each ride, a general check of the bicycle is important. Be sure it is mechanically ready to take you on your adventure. The most important item to check on your mountain bike is its stopping power. The standard brakes on a bicycle are very small and inefficient when you really think about it. They generally work by clinching the rim of the wheel tight enough to slow it down. The problem is that there is a great deal of momentum when the weight of the rider, bike, and carry-ons are moving at speed. To stop or slow down this inertia, the very small brake pads must very tightly rub on the wheel creating enough friction to displace that forward energy. A by-product of this friction is heat that causes fast wearing of the brake pads. They also loose their ability to grip as they heat up (partly the heat, partly the rims get coated with lost brake pad material and trail goop). This makes it doubly important to check and maintain your bike's braking system as best that you can. Be sure that the brake cables are pre-stretched, adjusted, and securely fastened. The pads should be clean, properly aligned and replaced often. They are inexpensive parts that can be easily replaced.

Some riders beef up their brakes with assisting mechanisms that give a mechanical advantage over standard stock brakes. There are support rings that add rigidity to the brake support brackets as well as brakes with internal mechanical advantages to aid in stopping.

Disc brakes are new to mountain bikes. They are heavier

than standard brakes but incredibly effective. The newest models have been adapted to the front wheel and are much lighter and very efficient. Disc brakes may someday be the norm for mountain bikes but now only are commonly used on tandem bicycles.

Small changes of riding habits can also make a difference in braking. Remember, the real stopping power of a bicycle is the front brake. The rear brake helps to maintain a true course but the front brake does the main work. That may sound surprising but much of your forward motion is weighing down the front of the bike when stopping. Its rather tricky at first to gauge how much force should be applied to the front brake without doing a nose stand or a handlebar flip. Speed on a bike is grand but out of control speed on a bike is a disaster about to happen. By anticipating your need to slow down, the chances of over-use of the front brake can be avoided. A tip is to shift your weight back on the saddle when braking to take some of the weight off the front tire. It even helps to lower the saddle on extended descents in order to shift weight back as much as possible. Some riders almost sit on the rear tire in order to keep their center of gravity back to aid in braking control on the steepest sections.

Here's the catch on steep downhill runs. No matter how far back on the bike you go, most of the stopping power and weight is still on the front tire. Learn to squeeze that front brake *after* applying the rear brake to assure that momentum won't carry you over the handlebars. This may sound complicated but after a few trial stops its easy to see how its done without mishap. The key is to be in control at all times. Its best to take it slow while you are practicing your skills of braking and stopping.

Gearing is an important part to check on your mountain bike. Most production bikes are set up for light climbing for someone with strong legs. Most mountain bikes have 3 chain rings in front and a rear "freewheel" of 6 or 7 gears in the back. Most new bikes are only adequate for short efforts to power your way to the top of a small incline.

In the mountains of Colorado, the climbs seem to never end. The steepness of the climb may not always be the culprit in stealing your energy. The length of climb can be just as devastating to your legs if you are pushing a "too large gear". (That's techno-bicycle talk that I've never really understood. It means that your *gear ratio* is very large.) Sure a large gear ratio (large chain ring gear/small freewheel gear) can propel you faster than those old "whimpy" gear combinations but just how long can you sustain the energy output before going into anaerobic debt or injuring your knees? "Its not how fast you get to the top, its just that you got there" (Author).

With proper technique, a minimum of tire slippage will occur when using the combination of the smallest (chain ring) gear in front and largest (freewheel) gear in back that your bike will handle. That not only saves you energy for enjoying the ride but lessens the impact of your tires on the trail. Gears for the front chain rings in the range of 24 or less teeth with a large rear freewheel gear of lets say 48 teeth will help propel you over the meanest of climbs. There are even after-market 4th chain rings available for real low down climbing power. Why grunt your way to the top of a climb when you can enjoy the ride at a steady (high spinning) pace? Save your energy for enjoying the ride not fighting it.

The jury is still out about putting "baskets" or toe clips

on the pedals. Some riders feel that their feet cannot get out of the toe clips fast enough in a tight situation. The same applies to the new clip pedal system for mountain bikes where the shoe snaps into a pedal device that holds the shoe in place. There are distinct advantages to both schools of thought but to have your foot at the most efficient placement over the axle of the pedal at all times is very important. The best advice I have heard is to have your foot unrestricted and out of any of the clips on tricky descents just in case a quick exit becomes necessary.

Some thought should be given to the type of tires to use on a mountain bike. First things first, where do you plan on riding? The jeep trails and back roads require a minimum of traction so a narrower profile, smoother tread design will be adequate. In those conditions choose a tire that will allow smooth rolling over hard surfaces and a higher inflation pressure for less rolling resistance.

For the bikers that will be riding in the real rugged outback, chose a tire with an aggressive tread pattern. Riders are now looking at tires with two designs for the front and rear. The front tire does the steering so more center tread is needed for cornering without slipping. The rear tire needs good gripping power tread so that it does not slip under demand. Although mountain bike tires can do some impact to trails, it can be lessened with the use of proper tires for the conditions and proper technique. However, there are no proper tires for muddy conditions in the High Country. Don't ride when you will damage the trail!

Mountain bikes can be outfitted with many special pieces of equipment such as shock absorbers or suspension systems to lessen the impact of difficult terrain. Items that add to your comfort for riding in the High Country will add to the enjoyment of the experience.

The number one personal safety item for any ride in the High Country is a properly fitted helmet. Wear it every minute that bike is moving. Accidents can and do happen without warning in the backcountry. A human head is no match for the hard granite rock that abounds throughout the High Country. Helmets are now made with excellent ventilation, a comfortable snug fit, some come with visors, and most are very light. They will also shade your head from the intense sunshine of the higher altitudes.

A good fitting pair of shoes with stiff soles will make each stroke on the pedal more efficient. It can be surprising how much of the downward force of each pedaling stroke is absorbed by tennis shoes used for general use. Real bicycle shoes transfer far greater energy into your peddling than tennis shoes. Special mountain bike shoes have aggressive treads for the times when walking/carrying the bike becomes necessary.

The thought of wearing those shiny lycra tight fitting bicycling shorts may not appeal to casual mountain bikers. To many the "Day-Glo look" just doesn't look right out in the beautiful High Country filled with the natural wonders of alpine flowers and evergreens. There are many highly functional mountain bike clothes that do work quite well without self-illuminating materials. The slightly padded shorts, and padded gloves made especially for bicycling can make a bumpy ride more comfortable. A bicycling shirt with the pockets in the back will allow easy access to simple items needed along the trail.

The last item I would suggest is to wear eye protection at all times. The tires of mountain bikes can throw small stones as well as dirt and mud. At any speed an insect might get lodged in an eye causing temporary loss of vision. I would suggest having clear lenses for cloudy days (a rarity in summer in Steamboat Springs) and quality sunglasses with 100% UV protection for most riding conditions.

The remains of an old cabin can be found along Hot Springs Trail. Many of the trails in this guide will pass the relics of the old days of miners and homesteaders. Please respect these old historic sites and let them "rest in peace".

THE MOUNTAIN BIKE AND NATURE

Is it possible to really see the Great Outdoors on a mountain bike? Of course it is! If fact, a good rider will be so inconspicuous and non-threatening that quite often bicycle riders will see much more wildlife than walkers or hikers will. Why, you ask? Because mountain bikes can be quieter, quicker, and can carry you to areas far beyond the normal day traveler. Mountain bikes can be ridden low-impact style without tearing up the scenery and serenity.

Practice skills that allow near silent biking. Quick shifting, easy pedaling cadence, and soft tires can be tools to come across wildlife before they see you. Be especially observant when entering open areas. There may be anything present from an elk to a coyote wandering the space. Large animals such as elk or mule deer will often "freeze" in place while you pedal by, if you are a quiet biker.

The High Country is a great place to see large wildlife. Recently logged areas often have a high density of aspen growing which is a favorite food of mule deer and elk. The areas of "dark timber" made up of spruce and fir trees are favorite places for mid-summer elk. Look for them resting by day and along the edges of the timber in the early mornings or late evenings.

The edges between forest and open areas are place to see the abundant bird life of the mountains. Some of the residents are Stellar's jay, gray jay, raven, mountain bluebirds, and the blue grouse. Birds of prey such as golden eagles, cooper's hawk, and kestrels are often spotted. The treat of early summer is the abundant and noisy little broad-tailed hummingbirds. They can be seen feeding in the meadows of spring wildflowers. A favorite food of this bird is the nectar of the Colorado Columbine, the state flower.

Most streams have beaver activity in the High Country. Look near the beaver lodges for adults or young out in the morning sunshine. Beaver are active all summer long feeding on aspen and willow shoots. It can also be fun to watch the brook trout rising to feed on insects on the surface of the ponds created by beaver dams. There may be other wildlife around the ponds such as nesting ducks, a mink, or you may even have a close encounter with a moose.

Mountain bikes are truly versatile vehicles that can carry more than just you. Why limit your experience to just the effort of biking alone? You can take along fishing equipment, cameras, binoculars, picnics, or another person on a tandem bicycle.

Bring along a camera, or a sketch pad to record your impressions along the way. A pocket type instant camera (35mm preferred) will allow you to "relive" some of the scenery or encounters with the local natives like a marmot, or mule deer. Riding at top speed only gets you from place to place in a shorter amount of time. Biking in the High Country is *already being there*! Why rush to leave where you came to be in the first place?

If you pick a destination, try to arrive with enough time to really enjoy the surroundings. It seems so often that it is only after you have stopped for a while that the real activities of the area come to life. If your presence is a nonthreatening one, animals become curious about you being out there on their home turf. I have had deer come up nose to nose in an attempt to figure out who or what was the newcomer in their neighborhood. Marmots and picas will resume their busy work once they feel safe.

Bring along a complete picnic lunch in order to take the time to drink in the surroundings of the High Country. Be considerate to others and make sure you pack out whatever you brought in. It is wonderful to experience a natural setting without litter scattered about.

Biking in the High Country is a special way to see and interact with Nature. The lakes are teeming with trout, Spring wildflowers last until mid-summer, the aspen turn golden in the fall, and the memory of the breath taking scenery never goes away when put on film.

The Author with a nice cutthroat trout. There are many lakes in the backcountry which may provide for some fishing excitement. (This trout was released back into the High Country lake).

SURVIVAL OF THE FITTEST?

Perhaps it should be survival of the prepared. No matter how fit or ready you may feel for a trip into some wild place, it really comes down to how prepared are you? Mountain biking is a wonderful way to visit special places away from the busier crowded trails. However, it is all to often forgotten that this new found mobility will carry you much farther away from where you could normally walk out if you got in trouble. It is also a longer distance for someone to come and get you in case of an accident. That means that some forethought is required about where you are going and what to do in case something goes wrong.

Traveling into the backcountry or any place beyond an hour's walk requires some preplanning. Mountain bikes can carry you to places that few others reach. That is a great advantage to the sport but also makes one more responsible for your own welfare. If you bike beyond where the average person goes then it is up to you to take care of yourself. It takes very little equipment to be prepared for most of the minor problems that can arise in cruising the backcountry. It is so important to take care of the minor things before they become major problems.

Become weather wise before departing. Nearly every afternoon in the summer holds a chance for a high mountain thunderstorm. That will mean heavy localized rains, possible strong winds, and deadly lightning. Be very conscience of open exposed locations once a storm has built up. Lone trees and high points are natural locations for lightning strikes. It is best to plan your travel times to avoid the highest areas in the late afternoons when storms are most common.

A safe and enjoyable trip means that you must stay comfortable, stay hydrated, and stay in control. There are 3 basic things that you want to be able to take along with you whenever you venture into the backcountry on a mountain bike. First, take along enough water (or means of purifying it) to last the whole trip. Second, take along bike repair tools and necessary supplies to handle the simple breakdowns. Third, take along a prepared self-rescue kit. With these three basic items along your on your trip, you are prepared to handle the simple problems and can spend more time enjoying your ride.

First, to take along enough water for the whole venture into the wilds seems easier than in truth. We are made up of nearly 80% water. The body needs that vast amount of water to function properly. When exercising, in any temperature, the body will cast off tremendous reserves of water as sweat or just expired as water vapor in your breath. In theory, that water should be replaced at a rate equal to the loss in order to maintain an equilibrium.

This is nearly impossible. Experienced bikers will drink long before they feel thirsty. A loss of water in the body will make you less efficient in strength and less efficient in judgments. Out in the backcountry is no place to be less sharp.

Carrying enough water to maintain that equilibrium just isn't practical when mountain biking. At 8 pounds per gallon, there is just so much water that one can carry along on a bike before it becomes counter-productive to the ride. In riding at higher elevations, it is not unusual to need a gallon of liquid a day to ride because of the altitude and dryness of the air.

The solution is to carry as much water as comfortable

then supplement along the route. A little preplanning with a map will show where sources of water will be such as springs, lakes and streams, or campgrounds. Most experienced mountain bikers never pass up a chance to refill their water supplies.

All water from the wild should be treated before consumption. It is a sad but true state that the little buggers that make you very sick may be found in all surface water sources in North America. You just cannot be certain of the source of even clear mountain springs, as it may have just gone underground a mile away after going through a high country pasture. It takes years of natural filtration to clean water. The safe thing to do is to take precautions with all surface water. There are many products that chemically or mechanically remove the offending parasites and bacteria from the water making it safe to take along on your ride. Pictures and memories are much more fun to take home than a case of Giardia, a nasty intestinal parasite.

The second essential item to take with you is a tool kit to repair the most common of bicycle breakdowns. You would feel pretty foolish to find yourself with a flat tire and no spare tube or patch kit while 10 miles away from help. Road bikers have carried supplies for years as they know that it only takes 10 minutes to get back on the road after a flat tire.

Well, think how silly you would be if you find yourself pushing your shiny new expensive bike back to the starting line just because you didn't even bring a $1.00 patch kit to fix a flat tire with you. Bikes are only mechanical devices and do break down occasionally.

If you are on an extended ride, bring that much more of a cross section of tools to take care of the things that duct tape won't fix. Talk to your local bike shop to assist you with picking out the most essential tools to take along. If you are riding with a group, the tools can be spread out among the party. With a wider selection of tools along, you can do a complete repair to last longer that just "ducking" the repair. Although it is suggested to never ride alone, the joys of solitude and interacting with nature on a solo trip are very rewarding. Just a little more discretion is required to be more conscience of the risks of your actions.

Make a point of taking a self-rescue kit along on every ride. This is especially important for solo riders. By preparing a simple self-rescue kit in advance it will always be available making it easier to take along with you. That saves you the time of hunting down the items each time and will encourage its use. Make it easy to carry...then you will care it. A stuff sack, small pouch, or case will work out fine. A kit that fits into a hip belt style fanny pack or even a small backpack can be carried along without a difficulty. The important thing to remember is that it is just as important to make it portable as it is to pack it. If it is hard to carry or you have to put it together every time before you go out, then chances are that you won't be taking it along. A self-rescue kit will not be of any value if left at home.

Be sure everything in this kit is needed and make sure you know how to use each item. For instance, you probably don't need a whole container of matches, only a few to get a fire started. It is wise to bring more than one method of fire starting as a backup. How many small bandages are enough? Why not take 6 of assorted sizes along instead of the entire container? How about a mini-flashlight?

Transparent film cans are a great way to pack items in limited quantity and still see the contents. They are a good place to put bandages, a small tube of antiseptic, mole skin, and some safety pins. An easy reminder of the contents of a container is to label it. In times of need the last thing you want to do is to have to really hunt for the needed items.

Pack a plastic poncho. They can be purchased for under a dollar at discount stores. Find an orange poncho if you can. It isn't safe to be invisible on a rainy day. The animals don't mind and if you are on a road the drivers will give you a wider clearance if they clearly see you out there.

A little nutrition goes along way. Find room for some edibles in your self-rescue kit. There are small items like wrapped hard candy that won't melt in the summer's heat and provide a boost of energy. Take along a couple of those nutritional bars such as "Power Bars"®. They digest well if you are actively riding and they feel like something substantial if you have to stop for a period of time due to an injury or problem.

The basic plan in making a self rescue kit should be to figure out what you would need in the area where you are traveling if you could not make it back to your vehicle or stopping place as you were intending to do. There are two phases of planning here. Where are you riding and what are the weather considerations during the trip. A trip to the Rocky Mountain region in any season can have changable weather. The bike trip may start as a bright sunny day but change to snow by mid-afternoon. Summer days can also start out clear and blue only to change to strong thunder showers with dangerous lightning. It is best to know what is the expected forecast of weather then be prepared for that *and* the unexpected.

Shelter is one of the greatest needs both on extended trips and for the unplanned overnight stay. A shelter can be created very easily with one or two of the pocket sized emergency blankets (thin foil blankets). They will keep you dry, and help retain some of your body heat. They are so small that every member of you group should have one. They also come in handy during an accident. A typical reaction of the body due to trauma is to cool down. This is a form of shock that can become a major problem. Injured parties should be kept warm to help minimize the effects of the trauma. A foil blanket will assist in forming a temporary shelter either used simply as a blanket or as a sunshade (a rain tarp, too). Try to do anything that is needed to keep an accident victim's body temperature close to normal.

The little foil blankets are very inexpensive. Use one if you are cold while on a break late in the day. They can also be made into personal groundcloths or windbreaks. These little rescue blankets can be cut into an impromptu poncho, a torso warming insert in front of your jersey or even handle bar muffs. Their uses are considerable, their cost low, and the benefits high so go ahead and use them. They may be hard to repack but any heat you save while recharging for the last part of the trip will be well worth the investment. Besides, you can then recycle them for your vehicle's emergency kit.

A simple but very important addition to your self-rescue kit is a personal identification card. It will not only "prove" who the kit belongs to if left behind on the trail but will speak for you if you cannot. If there has been an accident that leaves you unable to communicate, a personal ID will quickly give your rescuers the needed information to contact your designated or necessary party for the situation. You can also add information such as medical alerts to this ID to assist medical personnel.

Personal identification cards may be created by yourself, then laminated. Take a note card and trim it to size, then add the required information such as contact phone numbers, emergency contact persons, or medical information. A more official personal ID may be acquired at the Colorado Drivers Examining Division. There is a small fee, but you will receive a permanent picture ID that is easily recognized.

Mountain bike riding into the backcountry is exciting and challenging. The goal of every mountain bike expedition or day ride should be to have a safe and enjoyable experience. Some preplanning will go a long way whether riding solo or with a group of friends. To make that trip safer and to help stabilize those unforeseen problems make it a practice to take along a self-rescue kit. That may make the difference between a simple problem and a major one for yourself or for your traveling companions. Know where you are going and know your abilities. Last of all, be sure to leave word behind of your itinerary for the trip and check back in when you return.

Basic Supplies for a Self Rescue Kit

1. First aid kit
   a. bandaids, compresses, athletic tape

2. Space blanket
   a. the thin foil, pocket size

3. Water purifying system
   a. tablets or mechanical system*

4. Plastic whistle
   a. (metal may freeze to lips when cold)

5. Food bars
   a. at least one for each person on the trip

6. TP and trowel

7. Waterproof matches, lighter

8. Fire starting materials
   a. treated sticks, fire ribbon paste

9. Gloves (in cooler weather)

10. Rope or twine
    a. used in shelter building
    b. 50' parachute cord

12. Surveyor's tape
    a. emergency trail marking or location of injured

13. T-Handle saw or lock blade folding saw

14. Hat for cool weather (or balaclava)

15. Compass and map (topographical preferred)

16. Roll of electrician's tape

17. Flashlight (AAA mini-light)

18. Cylume™ lighting stick

19. Sheet of heavy aluminum foil.

20. Insect repellent

21. Back up knife or multitool

22. Emergency sewing kit with fishhooks

23. Pencil and paper

24. Personal ID

25. Positive Mental Attitude- or "How to change an ordeal into an adventure!"

INTRODUCTION TO MAPS

The mountain bike routes in this guide were selected to provide a wide range of mountain biking experiences and to give a choice of skill and fitness level challenges. Some days may not be your best days for riding challenging trails or some trails may be just too technical for your expertise. Read the description and then make an informed choice of a trail to ride.

You will find some helpful features to guide your way through this trail guide. The mountian bike rating symbol is a way of rating each ride according to the skills and physical effort required. A key is listed later in this section. This is a generalized key as rated for a visitor to the Steamboat Springs area with some mountain bike experience. It is very difficult to rate a trail as conditions change season to season, and even day to day.

Be sure to take into account your own fitness level. You may be well rested and in fine shape one day then very "off" the next time out. If you are riding in a group, the slowest or least experienced of the group should dictate the speed of the whole group. It is a matter of courtesy and safety to be sure that everyone has a great ride and arrives together.

The distances shown for each route are reasonably ac-curate, but trails do get altered, conditions change, and even your riding style may affect the total distance ridden. There are always interesting side trails, lookouts, lakes, or other points of interest along each route. You are encour-aged to do some exploring along each trail.

A general listing is provided to aid in finding the closest restrooms (high priority), parking/shuttle parking, dining places (picnicking, campsites, general stores), and fuel supplies.

The maps in this section are only meant to be a brief outline of the trails. In the field, it often takes a topographical map and a compass to know exactly where you are. There are much better maps available from the US Geological Survey Office, US Forest Service, and well constructed maps from Trails Illustrated®. These are available at most local bike shops and sporting goods dealers.

Conditions can change drastically during a day's ride. The weather may prohibit completion of the intended route, so alternatives may need to be planned in the field. There is nothing wrong with shortening a route or changing plans when necessary. A good map will aid in decision making.

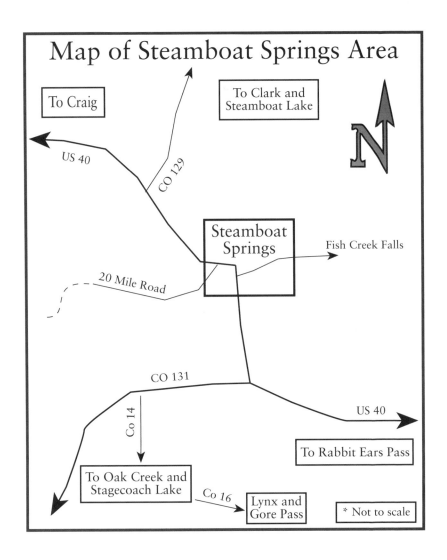

Map of Steamboat Springs Area

To Craig

To Clark and
Steamboat Lake

N

US 40

CO 129

Steamboat
Springs

Fish Creek Falls

20 Mile Road

CO 131

Co 14

US 40

To Rabbit Ears Pass

To Oak Creek and
Stagecoach Lake

Co 16

Lynx and
Gore Pass

* Not to scale

Key to Mountain Bike Route Rating System:

Fairly easy ride without hard climbs or descents. Family rides for all members with 2 wheelers.

Moderate rides with some climbing and easy descents. Mostly lower altitude (under 8000') and mostly low traffic gravel roads or 2 track trails.

Moderate rides with steep sections both up and brake testing downs. Must have acquired mountain bike handling skills to stay on trails varying from jeep trails to single tracks.

Difficult trails with sections of strenuous heart pounding climbs and brake testing descents. Altitude and obstacles make these challenging rides for the well prepared, experienced rider.

X 5 These would be **expert only** trails. Ones that require concentration, stamina, lack of fear, and a good insurance policy. These trails do exist in the Steamboat Springs area but are not in the intended scope of this book. Ask a local for details about their favorite "kamikaze course".

Buffalo Park Road

Rated:

Location: On US 40; Rabbit Ears Pass

Length: Nearly unlimited round trip distance. The route is 30 miles (one way) to Gore Pass to the South. Return on same route.

Elevation: 9400′ with minor grades at stream crossings. Buffalo Park is at 9200′.

Difficulty: Easy ride unless long distances are rode. Buffalo Park is approximately 11.5 miles one way.

Highlights: Differing habitats along the route make this an interesting ride. Buffalo Park once had woodland buffalo roaming there. Look for elk and deer.

Directions to Trailhead: Take US 40 out of Steamboat Springs toward Rabbit Ears Pass. Look on the right 1 mile past the Dumont Lake turnoff (where the Rabbit Ears Peaks are located) for a Forest Service sign for Buffalo Park. This is FR 100. Parking is found 100 yards from the US 40 intersection on the right.

Support and Facilities: Parking area is provided. Nearest restrooms at Dumont Lake Day Use Area/Campground. Fuel and food supplies in Steamboat Springs.

Maps of Area: Trails Illustrated® – Steamboat Springs South & Yampa Gore Pass / Routt National Forest

Buffalo Park Road

Description of Trail: Start at the parking area near US 40. Follow FR 100 as long as you care, with thought of returning the same route. Although this is a fairly well maintained gravel road it is lightly traveled. It is advised to plan on your rides in the mornings as dust and traffic do pick up in the afternoons in the summer.

There are no easy alternate routes for a return but diversions onto side logging access roads may prove to be interesting.

Map:

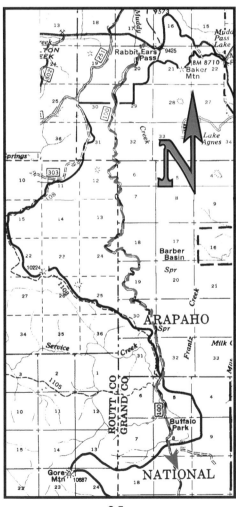

Buffalo Pass Road

Rated:

Location: North of Steamboat Springs; Strawberry Park.

Length: 11 miles from Strawberry Park Road to Summit Lake, the top of the Pass.

Elevation: 7000´ to 10,300´

Difficulty: This is a rocky, bumpy ride both ways. It will require strong legs for the ascent, and good braking skills on the descent. Afternoon motor vehicle traffic.

Highlights: Easy access to beautiful vistas. This is an excellent route in the fall with the aspens in their golden splendor.

Directions to Trailhead: Head North out of Steamboat Springs on 7th Street to Strawberry Park. Turn right onto Buffalo Pass Road. Parking is available just inside the National Forest boundary on the right side of the road.

Support and Facilities: No toilets near parking area. Dry Lake and Summit Lake campgrounds have toilets. Water at the campgrounds is not always available. Fuel and food available in Steamboat Springs.

Maps of Area: Trails Illustrated® – Clark, Buffalo Pass / Routt National Forest

Buffalo Pass Road

Description of Trail: Follow Buffalo Pass Road until you reach the summit. Along the route, there will be many vistas of the Yampa Valley and beyond. The road is rocky, and often soft at the higher elevations until July. Side trips at Dry Lake Campground's Soda Creek Trail (2 miles) or other 2-tracks are available.

The descent from the top of the pass can be a test for shock absorbers and breaking power. Motor vehicles are common on this route so caution is advised.

Map:

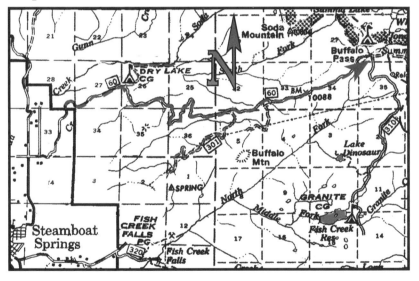

Coulton Creek Loop

Rated:

Location: North of Steamboat Springs; East of Clark

Length: A 10 mile loop. 8 Miles of off-road mostly single track & 2 miles on gravel road.

Elevation: 7800´ to 8600´

Difficulty: Moderate efforts on climbs and descents. Some sections may require pushing bike up grades especially if soft.

Highlights: After initial climbing, the trail gets nicer and nicer. This is what single track biking should be like everywhere. Note USFS innovative water bars on trail. Coulton Creek Canyon.

Directions to Trailhead: Head West from Steamboat Springs to Elk River Road (CO 129) one mile out of town on US 40. Turn North toward Clark and Steamboat Lake. Just North of Clark will be Seedhouse Road (FR 400). Turn right on Seedhouse Road for 4 miles to FR 429. Parking is on the left. An alternative parking area is one mile further on Seedhouse Road at the Hinman Day Use Area.

Support and Facilities: Parking only at the trailhead. One mile East is the Hinman Day Use Area and Campground on FR 440. Fuel and food supplies available at the Clark Store in Clark.

Maps of Area: Trails Illustrated® – Hahn's Peak / Routt National Forest

Coulton Creek Loop

Description of Trail: Head up TR 1188 climbing the first 1/2 mile for a fine view of Coulton Creek Canyon. The trail is an improved single track with mandatory switchbacks. It continues through varying habitats of forest and field to intersect the "cut-off trail" TR 1188A. You may wish to continue on TR 1188 until it fades 2 miles further up a beautiful valley. TR 1188A is a short 1.5 miles to intersect Hinman Creek Trail TR 1177. Turn right for a downhill ride. Watch for small Hinman Lake on the right. Cross Hinman Creek to intersect FR 330 for a final 2 track descent to Seedhouse Road. Turn right to complete loop.

Map:

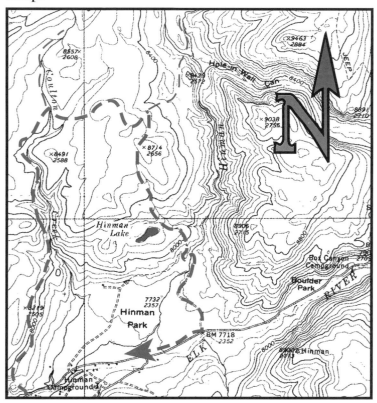

Diamond Park Road

Rated:

Location: North of Steamboat Springs; East of Clark

Length: 7.5 miles one way. This is the easiest option. See No.Elk River Loop for alternate routes to and returning from Diamond Park.

Elevation: 8000´ to 8800´. Mostly rolling terrain.

Difficulty: Fairly easy 2-track ride with one stream crossing. This is a good altitude acclimation ride. Can be a family ride but lengthy. May be soft at times.

Highlights: Very scenic from start to finish. If ridden slow, deer or an occasional elk may be seen. Diamond Park has some scenic old log buildings (all on private land).

Directions to Trailhead: Take US 40 west out of Steamboat Springs. Turn right onto CO 129 toward Clark and Steamboat Lake. Turn right on Seedhouse Road just North of Clark. Travel 8 miles East until you see FR 431. Parking is provided at this intersection just off Seedhouse Road.

Support and Facilities: Seedhouse Campground is 1/2 mile further East on Seedhouse Road where restrooms and water is available. Fuel and food supplies are available at the Clark Store in Clark.

Maps of Area: Trails Illustrated® – Hahn's Peak / Routt National Forest

Diamond Park Road

Description of Trail: Start from Seedhouse Road on FR 431. There is a brief initial climb but the rest is just rolling 2-track. The road is shared with off-road motorized vehicles but few venture on this often difficult (not so for mt. bikes) road. Turn right at the Farwell Mountain (FR 409) intersection to head for Diamond Park. There is one stream crossing which usually requires wading across. Diamond Park is a staging access to the Zurkel Wilderness. Enjoy a view or a walk but do not ride into the designated wilderness zone. Return via the same route.

Map:

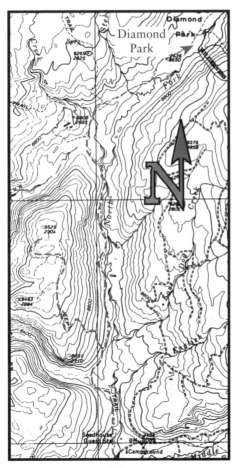

Dumont Lake Loop

Rated:

Location: South and East of Steamboat Springs; Rabbit Ears Pass

Length: 11 miles

Elevation: 9400´ to 10,200´

Difficulty: Moderate ride due to altitude and length. Almost all on 2-track with a short return on pavement.

Highlights: Exceptional views of Dumont Lake. Early summer wildflowers.

Directions to Trailhead: Take US 40 South out of Steamboat Springs toward Rabbit Ears Pass. At approximately 20 miles, look for the Dumont Lake turn off. This road was an older section of US 40. Park either at the Day Use Area or continue the 1/4 mile to the stone monument. The trailhead is 100 yards directly North. It is often gated closed to motor vehicles until late-June due to snow melt.

Support and Facilities: Toilets are available at the Day Use Area. The campground has water. Closest fuel and food supplies available in Steamboat Springs.

Maps of Area: Trails Illustrated® – Steamboat Springs South / Routt National Forest

Dumont Lake Loop

Description of Trail: Start at the Rabbit Ears Pass Monument. Head North on FR 311. The trail climbs quickly 600 feet in the first 2 miles. Then the effort is rewarded with outstanding views of Dumont Lake and snow-capped peaks in the distance. The trail intersects FR 313 at approximately 4.5 miles. It is not well marked but is in an open field and is closed to motor vehicles. Follow this somewhat bumpy 2-track back to US 40. It ends at a Highway Maintenance Garage area. Leave the access gate as found, then proceed as if this were private property the 100 yards to US 40. Turn left for the 1/2 mile return to the Dumont Lake turn-off. *NO parking or stopping in the State Highway Garage area.

Map:

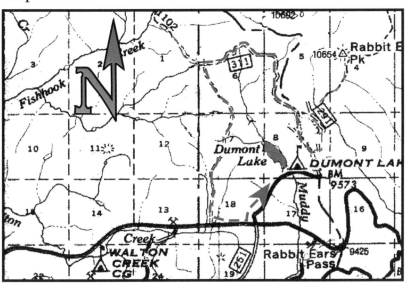

Elk Park Trail

Rated:

Location: North of Steamboat Springs; Strawberry Park Road

Length: 4.2 miles one way. Option for a side trip to Summit Park adds just over 5 miles.

Elevation: 7400′ to 8700′ to Elk Park
8400′ to 10,000′ to Summit Park

Difficulty: The initial climb will test your strength and ability. The side trail to Summit Park is quite challenging. The return downhill makes it all worthwhile.

Highlights: Pleasant views of the high country. Elk Park very nice in the fall. Summit Park is the source of the Hot Springs Creek (but not warm at the origin).

Directions to Trailhead: Turn North in Steamboat Springs at 7th street. Continue following signs to Strawberry Park, a valley just North of town. Continue on Strawberry Park Road until it turns to gravel. It is now Hot Springs Road. On the right, FR 314 is the route for this ride. Parking is provided 100 yards uphill on Hot Springs Road from this point. There is no parking available by the trailhead.

Support and Facilities: No toilet facilities available. Fuel and food supplies in Steamboat Springs.

Maps of Area: Trails Illustrated® – Steamboat Springs North / Routt National Forest

Elk Park Trail

Description of Trail: Start on FR 314 going uphill. It turns left after crossing a stream culvert. Then the real climb begins. This 2-track is open to 4 wheel drive vehicles and is often deeply rutted. At the 2.2 mile mark, the climbing part to Elk Park is over. The trail now crosses over Bear Creek, a short but wet crossing. To add an additional 5 miles, turn right to follow TR 1206 for an extended climbing ride to Summit Park. This is more difficult and all single track. Summit Park is just outside of the Zurkel Wilderness. A great place for a picnic. Elk Park is only 1.8 miles from the crossing. The 2-track ends at a hikers only trailhead.

Map:

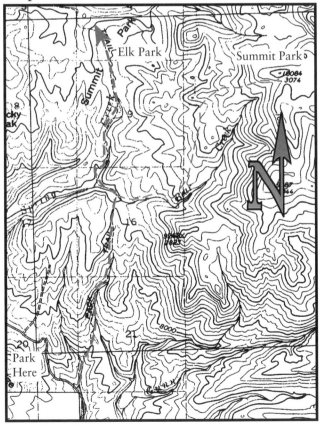

Elk Run Trail

Rated:

Location: Stagecoach State Recreation Area; South of Steamboat Springs; East of Oak Creek

Length: Trail: 5 miles; Loop around lake: 11.5 miles

Elevation: 7200´ to 7300´

Difficulty: The trail is fairly easy and well constructed. The loop around the lake requires on road sections not appropriate for young children.

Highlights: Scenic lake in wild sagebrush country. Deer, prairie dogs, and badgers may be found along the route.

Directions to Trailhead: Head South out of Steamboat Springs on US 40. At about 4 miles turn right on CO 131. Turn left on Co 14 toward Stagecoach Lake. Park within Stagecoach Lake State Park in designated day use areas. A Colorado State Park Motor Vehicle Permit is required but at a nominal cost for a day pass. If you are riding only on the trail, park near the dam on Co 18.

Support and Facilities: Toilets are available in the main camp/day use area of Stagecoach Park. Fuel and food available in Oak Creek.

Maps of Area: Trails Illustrated® – Steamboat Springs, Rabbit Ears Pass / Routt National Forest / Stagecoach State Recreation Area
*Note: Reservoir not shown on older maps

Elk Run Trail

Description of Trail: The trail is on the South shore of Stagecoach Lake. It starts at the dam and ends on Co 16, a paved road. The surface is hard packed gravel and easy to ride. This portion is recommended for families. A loop route may be created by starting at the Day Use area or marina. Head North to Co 18, the road along the Northern shore of the lake. Turn right at the dam, follow the trail until it ends on Co 16. The paved road return to the main parking area is a moderately busy road with no area or shoulders for bicycle traffic. It is not recommended for young bicycle riders.

Map:

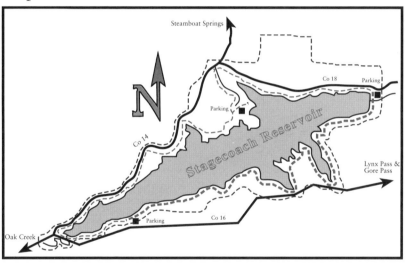

Fishcreek Reservoir Loop

Rated:

Location: Buffalo Pass; Northeast of Steamboat Springs

Length: 12 miles

Elevation: 9800′ to 10,400′

Difficulty: Easy to moderate effort on good roads and single track sections. Because of altitude and changeable weather, not suitable to inexperienced riders.

Highlights: Outstanding high country ride. Long Lake is very scenic and swimmable in summer. The Divide Trail portion is very enjoyable to single-trackers.

Directions to Trailhead: Tough route for passenger vehicles. Head North out of Steamboat Springs on Strawberry Park Road. Turn right on Buffalo Pass Road (CO 60). It is a 11 long miles to the top of the pass. Turn right on FR 310 and continue for 5 miles to the campground at Fishcreek Reservoir. Park here and head South on FR 310A for 1/4 mile to the start of the single track TR 1102.

Support and Facilities: Toilets available at Fishcreek Reservoir Campground. Fuel and food available in Steamboat Springs. *Note: This reservoir and campground is scheduled for upgrade work.

Maps of Area: Trails Illustrated® - Steamboat Springs South, Steamboat Springs North / Routt National Forest

Fishcreek Reservoir Loop

Description of Trail: Start at reservoir then head South on FR
310A to end of road. The trail TR 1102 starts here. The single track
section ends on a gravel service road to Long Lake at 2 miles from the
start. Continue on the single track on the east end of Long Lake. It
heads gradually uphill to intersect TR 1100, the Divide trail. At this 4
way intersection of trails, you may wish to view Round and Percy
Lakes only a half mile away on TR 1134. To continue on the
Fishcreek Loop, turn left on TR 1100 and follow this single track 6
miles until it intersects FR 310. Turn left and enjoy the pleasant
downhill run of 3 miles to the finish.

Map:

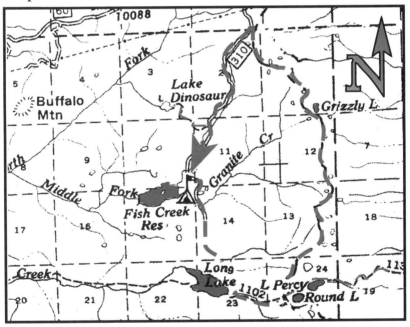

Gore Creek Loop

Rated:

Location: East of Toponas; Gore Pass; Lynx Pass; CO 134

Length: 14 miles

Elevation: 8700´ to 9700´

Difficulty: Easy Forest Road Route except for length.

Highlights: Very low traffic Forest Roads through varying habitats. Elk and deer country.

Directions to Trailhead: Head South from Steamboat Springs on US 40. Turn right on CO 131 toward Oak Creek. Continue past Oak Creek on CO 131 to Toponas. Turn left on CO 134. Three miles past the Lynx Pass turn off look for FR 250 (Rock Creek Road) on the left. Park at the Day Use lot 150 yards on the left off FR 250.

Support and Facilities: Toilets are nearby Lynx Pass, Blacktail, and Gore Campgrounds. Fuel and food available in Toponas. Restaurants in Yampa or Oak Creek.

Maps of Area: Trails Illustrated® – Yampa, Gore Pass / Routt National Forest

Gore Creek Loop

Description of Trail: The entire route is on low traffic Forest Roads. Please be aware of possible traffic especially on FR 250. Start on FR 250 for 2.8 miles to Gore Creek Road (FR 243). Turn right for a gentle 7 mile climbing grade along side of the Gore Creek valley. This stretch is a beautiful backcountry road. Turn right on FR 241 for a 3.7 mile descent to complete the loop.

This is a pleasant family level ride for those capable of going the 14 mile distance. The only challenge (aside from the 1000' elevation gain) will be counting deer, bluebirds, and looking at all the animal tracks along the sides of the road.

Map:

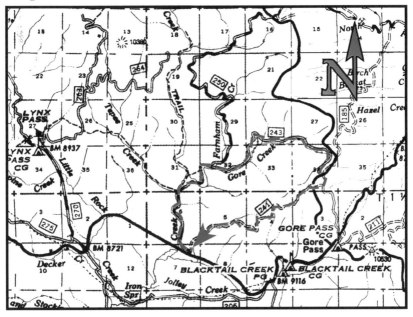

Greenville Loop

Rated:

Location: North of Steamboat Springs; Clark

Length: The Loop itself is 9 miles. Starting in Clark makes a 14 mile round trip. Starting at Hinman Day Use Area is a 15 mile round trip.

Elevation: The Loop: Ranges from 8000′ to 8600′ Clark: 7300′ Hinman Day Use Area: 7700′

Difficulty: Overall an easy ride except for the length. The climb from Clark to the Loop can be tough for beginners.

Highlights: Marvelous forested 2-track. The aspens make this a superior ride in the autumn foliage time. Side trips available to Big Creek Ridge and Big Creek.

Directions to Trailhead: Head west out of Steamboat Springs on US 40 then turn right on CO 129 toward Steamboat Lake and Clark for 18 miles. There are 3 trailhead parking areas. One at the Clark Store (with permission only), the second at the Hinman Day Use area (FR 440) off Seedhouse Road, or turn right on FR 440 and travel 2.6 miles to the FR 440/471 intersection. There is no parking available on the private land which borders FR 440 for the first 1.2 miles off CO 129.

Support and Facilities: No toilets available near any trailhead except for the Hinman Day Use Area (Campground nearby). Fuel available at Clark. Food, ice cream, restaurant, and lodging in Clark.

Maps of Area: Trails Illustrated® – Clark, Buffalo Pass & Hahn's Peak / Routt National Forest

Greenville Loop

Description of Trail: All of this route is 2-track or gravel surface. If starting in Clark, follow FR 440 east for 2.6 miles to the FR 440 / FR 471 intersection. This will involve a 700′ elevation gain mostly in the last 1.5 miles. Follow FR 471 for about 4 mile to the gated FR 468 on the left. Follow FR 468 until it meets FR 441, a gravel road. Turn left, travel 1/2 mile then turn left again on FR 440 to complete the loop. There is a 1/2 mile section of FR 440 at 1.5 miles from the last intersection that is damp, grassy, and sometimes hard to follow. To start at Hinman Day Use Area, follow FR 440 for 3 miles up the grade to start the loop.

Map:

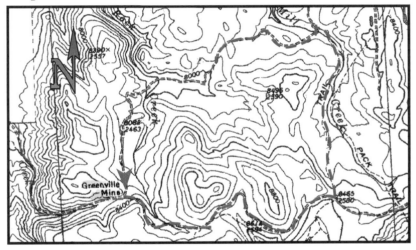

Hidden Lakes Loop

Rated:

Location: North side of Buffalo Pass; North of Steamboat Springs

Length: 14 mile loop

Elevation: 8500´ to 9300´

Difficulty: Moderate effort in the first 1.7 mile uphill section but most of this route is on good hard surfaced Forest Roads.

Highlights: Very low motor vehicle traffic makes this a good area for family rides. Colorado moose country as well as some logging activity on weekdays.

Directions to Trailhead: A) Head North out of Steamboat Springs on Strawberry Park Road. Turn right on Buffalo Pass Road (Co 60). Travel over Buffalo Pass and down the other side to Grizzly Creek Campground. (Note: this route NOT recommended for passenger vehicles) B) Take US 40 south out of Steamboat Springs over Rabbit Ears Pass. Turn left at Hwy 14 toward Walden. Turn left on Co 24 at Hebron. Follow this to Grizzly Creek Campground. (60mi)

Support and Facilities: Toilets and water available at Grizzly Creek and Hidden Lakes Campgrounds. If campground is full, please park in day use lot. Fuel and food available in Steamboat Springs or Walden.

Maps of Area: Trails Illustrated® – Clark, Buffalo Pass & Steamboat Springs South / Routt National Forest

Hidden Lakes Loop

Description of Trail: This loop utilizes 3 Forest Roads. Start at the Grizzly Lake Campground. Follow Buffalo Pass Road uphill 1.7 miles passing the return route. Turn left on FR 620 (Sawmill Creek Road). This will start a decent at the 3.5 mile mark. It is not technical but caution should be exercised. The FR 620 ends on Hidden Lakes Road (FR 20). Additional distance can be added to the right (its 6.5 miles to the end), but the main route turns left to return to Buffalo Pass Road in 6 miles. Plan on a stop at Hidden Lakes Campground along the way. It is a pretty spot for a break. Turn right on Buffalo Pass Road for the final descent.

Map:

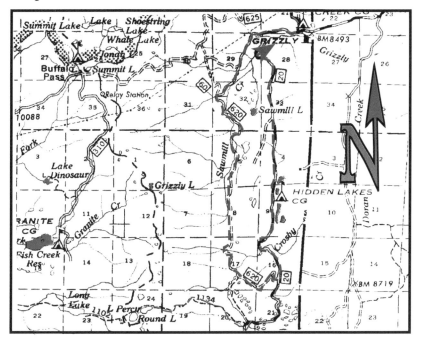

Hot Springs Trail

Rated:

Location: North of Steamboat Springs; Mad Creek Staging Area

Length: 3 miles one way

Elevation: 6800′ to 7400′

Difficulty: Moderate bike handling skills required as the trail is a narrow single track.

Highlights: The higher portion has a very remote feeling. The marvelous Strawberry Park Hot Springs at the Eastern trailhead.

Directions to Trailhead: Head West out of Steamboat Springs on US 40. Turn right or North on CO 129. At about 5 miles is the Mad Creek Staging area parking lot on the right. The trailhead is just South of this parking area. Cross Mad Creek and look to the left (East) for a 2-track heading uphill. This is FR 182. The trail makes an immediate right after the Forest Service gate.

Support and Facilities: A toilet is provided at the 40 car parking lot. Fuel and food supplies are available in Steamboat Springs. No potable water is found at the trailhead or along the route.

Maps of Area: Trails Illustrated® – Clark, Buffalo Pass / Routt National Forest

Hot Springs Trail

Description of Trail: Start on FR 128 just south of the CO 129
Mad Creek crossing. Turn right after the USFS gate on the narrow 2-
track. This part of the trail is an access through private land.
 Continue on this trail as it becomes a delightful single track along
Hot Springs Creek. At the 2 mile mark a pair of old cabins are along
the trail. The route now starts to climb the valley. There are some
pools along the trail that are usually warm enough to enjoy a quick
dip. The trail ends at the private concession at the Strawberry Park
Hot Springs. Return the same route or continue on FR 323 all the
way to Steamboat Springs (about 6 miles).

Map:

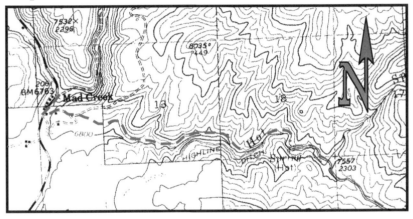

Mad Creek Trail

Rated:

Location: North of Steamboat Springs on CO 129

Length: 5 mile round trip (if extension is taken)

Elevation: 6700′ to 7100′

Difficulty: Easy to moderate effort required on the initial climb. Solid bike handling skills required due to steep canyon along side of trail.

Highlights: Very popular trail for bikers, hikers, and horsemen. Users share the trail with a courtesy for others. Great morning or evening ride.

Directions to Trailhead: Head West on US 40 from Steamboat Springs. Turn right on CO 129 toward Steamboat Lake and Clark. In 5 miles, look for the Mad Creek Staging Area on the right just after crossing Mad Creek. The trail starts on the North side of the parking lot.

Support and Facilities: A toilet is provided at the 40 car parking lot. Fuel and food supplies are available in Steamboat Springs. No potable water is found at the trailhead or along the route.

Maps of Area: Trails Illustrated® – Clark, Buffalo Pass / Routt National Forest

Mad Creek

Description of Trail: Start at the Mad Creek Staging Area. The first 200 yards is deceivingly steep, then assumes a more gradual climbing grade. Mad Creek canyon is beside the entire first part of this route. A gate marks the Mad Creek Park area. A Forest Service personnel cabin (The Mad House) is near the trail at this point.

An extension is on Swamp Park Trail (TR 1100), passing the cabin and continuing up the valley with Mad Creek a short distance to the right. The bike trail ends at a small irrigation ditch where Mad Creek finally comes closest to the trail. The Zurkel Wilderness is beyond but off-limits to mountain bikes. Return via the same route.

Map:

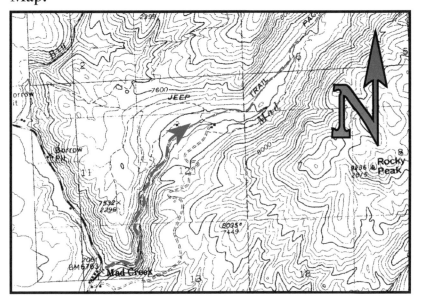

Mad Creek - Loop Routes

Rated:

Location: North of Steamboat Springs on CO 129

Length: Loop A: 6 mile round trip
Loop B: 7 mile round trip

Elevation: 6700′ to (A) 7400′ (B) 7500′

Difficulty: Loop "A": A sustained climb out of Mad Creek Park makes this a good workout. More advanced bike handling skills required on Loop "B".

Highlights: Very popular trail for bikers, hikers, and horsemen. Users should share the trail with a courtesy toward others. Great morning or evening ride as the extended loops can be difficult midday in hot weather.

Directions to Trailhead: Head West on US 40 from Steamboat Springs. Turn right on CO 129 toward Steamboat Lake and Clark. In 5 miles, look for the Mad Creek Staging Area on the right just after crossing Mad Creek. The trail starts on the North side of the parking lot.

Support and Facilities: A toilet is provided at the 40 car parking lot. Fuel and food supplies are available in Steamboat Springs. No potable water is found at the trailhead or along the route.

Maps of Area: Trails Illustrated® – Clark, Buffalo Pass / Routt National Forest

Mad Creek - Loop Routes

Description of Trail: Start at the Mad Creek Staging Area. A gate marks the Mad Creek Park area. A Forest Service personnel cabin (The Mad House) is straight ahead. Loop "A": Turn right at the next 2-track to coast down to a wooden bridge crossing Mad Creek. This is FR 128 which then climbs high above the valley. The decent on the other side returns you 100 yards south of the Mad Creek Staging Area. Loop "B": Turn left on TR 1140 to climb to the ridge top. There it intersects Red Dirt Trail (TR 1171). Turn left (West) and begin a quick, challenging decent to CO 129. Turn left on the paved road for the 1 mile return ride to the Mad Creek Staging Area.

Map:

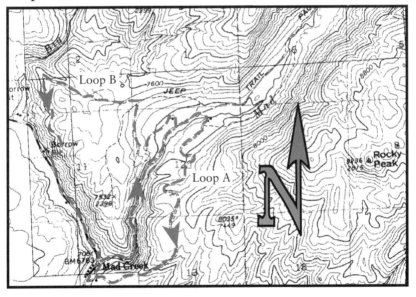

Midway Trail & Loop

Rated:

Location: Lynx Pass; Gore Pass; East of Toponas; Southeast of Stagecoach Lake State Park

Length: 25 miles

Elevation: 8700′ to 10, 200′

Difficulty: Long route with hard climbing grades, stream crossings, varied terrain. The trail is unmarked along High Rock Creek. Some wet sections.

Highlights: Varied trails from single tracks, 2-tracks, forest roads, to paved highway. The backcountry along High Rock Creek is very interesting. Elk country.

Directions to Trailhead: Take US 40 South from Steamboat Springs 3 miles to CO 131. Turn right and travel to Co. 16 toward Stagecoach Lake. On the South side of the lake is Co. 16/FR 270. Turn left (East) on this paved road. It later turns to gravel but continues to the Lynx Pass Campground. FR 263 is 1/4 mile past the campground. Turn left on FR 263 for 1/2 mile. Parking is on the road. An alternate route is CO 131 to Toponas, left on CO 134 to Lynx Pass Road (FR 270).

Support and Facilities: Toilets and water are available at the Lynx Pass Campground. Fuel and food are available in Oak Creek and Toponas.

Maps of Area: Trails Illustrated® – Yampa, Gore Pass / Routt National Forest

Midway Trail & Loop

Description of Trail: Follow either Tepee Creek trail or FR 463.
In 4 miles, FR 463 will cross the West Fork of Tepee Creek. Continue
for 3/4 mile to a 2-track to the right. This is unmarked but its the only
trail around. The 2-track descends to a clearing at High Rock Creek.
The Midway Trail follows the creek starting at this clearing (away
from the 2-track). In 1 mile, cross the creek and follow it downstream
on the single track. Turn left where the trail forks and another stream
joins. This again is unmarked. A logging road will intersect the trail in
1/2 mile. Turn right to FR 250. Turn right on FR 250. It is 8 miles to
CO 134. Turn right to return to FR 470 and finish.

Map:

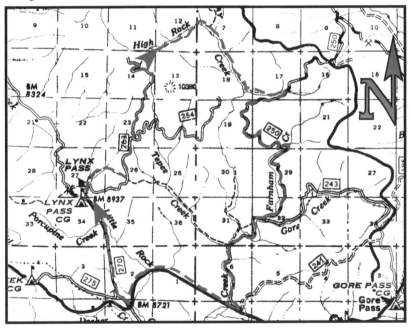

Morrison Divide Trail

Rated:

Location: Southeast of Stagecoach Reservoir; Lynx Pass

Length: 12 miles (18.5 with forest road return)

Elevation: 8900′ to 10,200′

Difficulty: Moderate effort with a few sustained climbs. The descent from the Slide area requires good bike handling skills.

Highlights: Very nice trail, well marked and maintained. Although open to off-road motorcycles and ATV's few are seen. Great views from the Slide Area. The Muddy Slide itself is of geological interest.

Directions to Trailhead: There are 2 "trailheads" on FR 270 but the preferred site is at Lynx Pass. Take US 40 South from Steamboat Springs 3 miles to CO 131. Turn right and travel to Co. 16 toward Stagecoach Lake. On the South side of the lake is Co. 16/ FR 270. Turn left (East) on this paved road. It later turns to gravel but continues to the Lynx Pass Campground. Park 100 yards short of the camp at the designated lot. It is 33 miles from Steamboat Springs to this trailhead.

Support and Facilities: Toilets and water are available at the Lynx Pass Campground. Fuel and food are available in Oak Creek and Toponas.

Maps of Area: Trails Illustrated® – Yampa, Gore Pass / Routt National Forest

Morrison Divide Trail

Description of Trail: This trail travels along a high ridge for most of its length until descending back to FR 270. The trail is a combination of wide single track, 2-tracks, old logging roads, and narrow single track. It climbs from the start, mostly on gentle grades to reach wonderful views and "The Slide". The geological wonder, "The Slide" or "Muddy Slide" is a curious wash out area where half a mountain is "missing". On a clear day, views of distant mountain ranges are possible, including the famous Rabbit Ears Peaks. The trail now descends on a twisty, but fun downhill run to FR 270. Turn right for the 6.5 mile gravel road return.

Map:

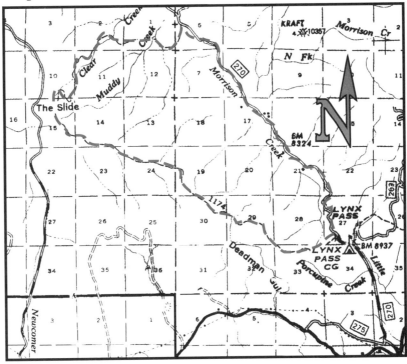

Nipple Peak - Short Loop

Rated:

Location: North of Steamboat Lake; Columbine

Length: Short Loop: 13.5 miles

Elevation: 8400´ to 8800´

Difficulty: The Forest Roads have easy grades; Connection single track TR 1156 is very challenging in sections.

Highlights: Nice backcountry route with exciting, mostly downhill single track section.

Directions to Trailhead: Take US 40 west out of Steamboat Springs to the CO 129 turnoff. Head North past Clark, Hahn's Peak Village, and Steamboat Lake. Continue to FR 486, turn left to the Hahn's Peak Lake. Day Use parking is provided. The short loop starts by returning on the camp access road to FR 487. The USFS gate on FR 487 is often closed until mid-summer to motor vehicles.

Support and Facilities: Toilets, water, and picnic tables are available at the Hahn's Peak Lake Day Use / Campground. Food, restaurant, lodging, and fuel available at Hahn's Peak Village.

Maps of Area: Trails Illustrated® – Hahn's Peak / Routt National Forest

Nipple Peak - Short Loop

Description of Trail: Start at the turn-off to Hahn's Peak Lake.
Head west on FR 487 for 3.1 miles. TR 1156 (Prospector's Trail)
crosses at this point. Left is the long loop and toward Slater Park.
Turn right on TR 1156 for a 5 mile single track adventure. A couple
sections may require carrying or guiding your bike down. The trail
ends on FR 488, a well maintained forest road. If you have the energy, head up to the end (2 miles) for good views and an enjoyable
descent back down. The return route is down FR 468 to its end on Co
129. Turn right and continue to FR 486 for the return to Hahn's Peak
Lake.

Map:

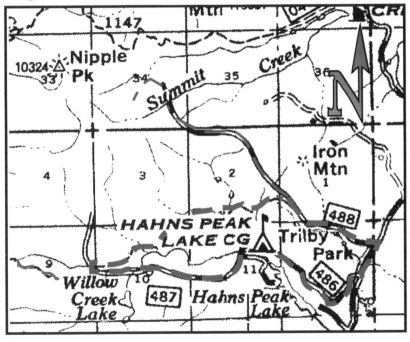

Nipple Peak - Long Loop

Rated:

Location: North of Steamboat Lake; Columbine

Length: 21 miles

Elevation: 8400′ to 9600′

Difficulty: Very long and difficult trail. Some walk or carry sections. Remote location requires preparation and planning. Advanced riders only.

Highlights: Outstanding views of Hahn's Peak, and Bear's Ears Peaks to the West. Well maintained trail system with extensions available.

Directions to Trailhead: Take US 40 west out of Steamboat Springs to the CO 129 turnoff. Head North past Clark, Hahn's Peak Village, and Steamboat Lake. Continue to FR 486, turn left to the Hahn's Peak Lake. Day Use parking is provided. The long loop starts by returning on the camp access road to FR 487. The USFS gate on FR 487 is often closed until mid-summer to motor vehicles.

Support and Facilities: Toilets, water, and picnic tables are available at the Hahn's Peak Lake Day Use / Campground. Food, restaurant, lodging,and fuel available at Hahn's Peak Village.

Maps of Area: Trails Illustrated® – Hahn's Peak / Routt National Forest

Nipple Creek - Long Loop

Description of Trail: Start at Hahn's Peak Lake. Head west on FR
487 for 3.1 miles. TR 1156 (Prospector's Trail) crosses at this point.
Right is the short loop. Turn left on TR 1156 and start climbing. A
saddle at 9300' (2 miles) offers nice views of Hahn's Peak and Bear
Ear's Peaks to the west. Continue downhill to TR 1147 junction.
Turn right (North) on TR 1147 for a 4 mile grind uphill to reach the
saddle (9600') near Nipple Peak. The next 4 miles descends to join FR
47, a 2-track, for the final descent to CO 129. Turn right and climb
on this all surface road bearing right at the next road. Pass through
Columbine, then to FR 486 to finish the loop.

Map:

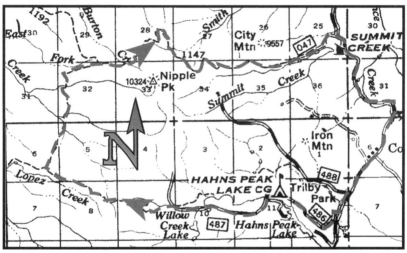

North Elk River Loop

Rated:

Location: North of Steamboat Springs; East of Clark; Seedhouse Road

Length: Loops of 11, 16, 22 miles.

Elevation: Trail starts 8000´ to 8600´. Road section starts 7200´.

Difficulty: Short loop is easiest with 2-track return. Long loop on TR 1177 is difficult with at least one carry section.

Highlights: Very scenic forested route. Single track sections challenging. Can usually see mule deer along the route.

Directions to Trailhead: All trail loops start and end on Seedhouse Road. From Steamboat Springs, take US 40 West to CO 129. Head North toward Steamboat Lake and Clark. Just past Clark, turn right on Seedhouse Road / FR 400. The first trail intersection is FR 468, the second FR 431, the third is FR 433. Suggested parking location is in the middle of your planned loop such as in Boulder Park.

Support and Facilities: Toilets available in Hinman or Seedhouse Campgrounds. Food, restaurant,and fuel available in Clark.

Maps of Area: Trails Illustrated® – Hahn's Peak / Routt National Forest

North Elk River Loop

Description of Trail: Preferred start is off Lost Dog Road, FR 433.
This is 1/4 mile past Seedhouse Campground. Parking at Boulder Park
or even Hinman Park will save a long road ride after such a great
backcountry experience. Take FR 433 about 1/3 mile to TR 1100 on
the left. Follow this old stock driving trail the 5 miles to Diamond
Park. Turn left on FR 431, cross Trail Creek then continue to the FR
431 / FR 409 junction. A FR 431 return is an 11 mile loop . Continue
about 1/3 mile on FR 409 to TR 1177. This is a tough, 7 mile backcountry trail to Seedhouse Road. An additional 6 miles may be added
at TR 1188A to Coulton Creek Trail.

Map:

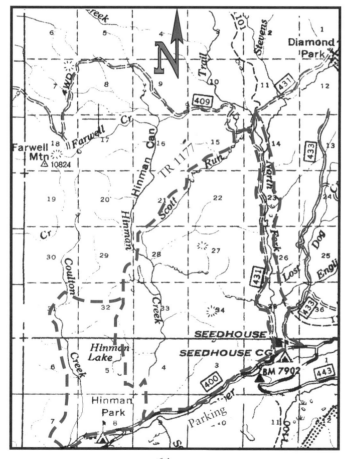

61

North Fish Creek

Rated:

Location: East of Steamboat Springs; Fish Creek Falls

Length: 6 mile round trip

Elevation: 7500′ to 7900′

Difficulty: Difficult initial climb and occasional walk sections. Mostly an easy 2-track trail to North Fish Creek.

Highlights: Outstanding view of Fish Creek Falls. Closest location to Steamboat Springs for pica watching. Old mining site along route.

Directions to Trailhead: In Steamboat Springs, turn North on 3rd Street. It jogs right, then proceeds uphill 4 miles to the Fish Creek Falls Day Use Area. Park at the main parking area at the end of the road or the long term lot 100 yards prior. The trail head is hard to see on the left (North) side of the road between the two lots. It is a 2-track angling up to the left. The trail marker is usually missing. *Note: Fish Creek Falls Trail (TR 1102) is *not* recommended for Mountain Bikes.

Support and Facilities: Toilets at the Fish Creek Falls Day Use Area. Food and fuel available in Steamboat Springs.

Maps of Area: Trails Illustrated® – Steamboat Springs South / Routt National Forest

North Fish Creek

Description of Trail: The initial 1/4 mile climb is a tough, switch-backing route. The reward is an outstanding view of Fish Creek Falls few visitors get to see. This is followed by a rock slide zone above and below the trail 50 yards further. This zone is the closest location to town to regularly see the pica, a rodent the size of a domestic gerbil. They are usually located first by their call, a high pitched "eek!". The 2-track trail continues through aspens, rocky outcrops, and open scrublands. An abandoned mine site is at the 2 mile mark. The trail finally descends to a crossing of North Fish Creek. Enjoy the site, then return by the same route. (Trail not maintained beyond the crossing).

Map:

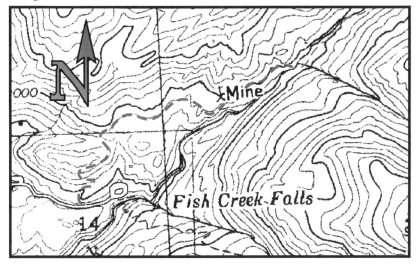

Percy Lake Loop - North

Rated:

Location: Buffalo Pass; North of Steamboat Springs

Length: 23 miles

Elevation: 8700′ to 10,300′

Difficulty: Moderate effort with extensive climb.

Highlights: Beautiful high country route. Lakes, streams, forests, mountain meadows.

Directions to Trailhead: Head North out of Steamboat Springs on Strawberry Park Road. Turn right on Buffalo Pass Road (CO 60)*. It is a long 11 miles to the top of the pass. Park at the Day Use area. *Tough route for passenger vehicles.

Support and Facilities: Toilets available at Summit Lake Campground. Fuel and food available in Steamboat Springs.

Maps of Area: Trails Illustrated® – Steamboat Springs South and Steamboat Springs North & Clark, Buffalo Pass / Routt National Forest

Percy Lake Loop - North

Description of Trail: Start at Summit Lake heading east on FR 310. In 1.5 miles TR 1100 will be on the left. Follow this single track to the 4-way intersection of Trails 1134 and 1102. Turn left on TR 1134 descending past Round and Percy Lakes. The trail ends on FR 20 / Hidden Lakes Road. Turn left (North) for 2 miles to FR 620. A left again will begin a short 2 mile climb, then it levels out for the next 3.5 miles. At the intersection with Co 60 / Buffalo Pass Road turn left for the final climb of 4.5 miles to the top of the pass and Summit Lake.

Map:

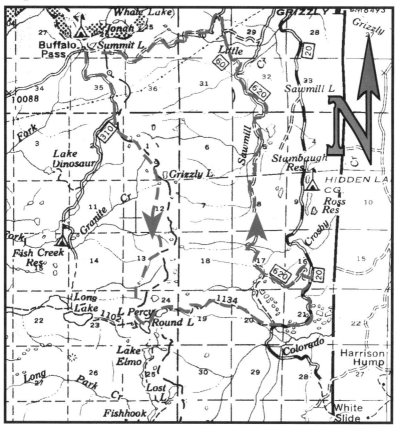

Rabbit Ears Peaks

Rated:

Location: South and East of Steamboat Springs; Rabbit Ears Pass

Length: 6 mile round trip

Elevation: 9600′ to 10,400′

Difficulty: Not a technical ride but altitude and grade make this challenging.

Highlights: Beautiful meadows, extensive vistas from the base of the Peaks.

Directions to Trailhead: Head South out of Steamboat Springs on US 40. Travel approximately 18 miles to the Dumont Lake turn-off. Turn left and continue to the Day Use Parking area or to the stone monument. The trail starts due North of the monument on FR 311.

Support and Facilities: Toilets and water available at Dumont Lake Day Use and Campground. Fuel and food supplies available in Steamboat Springs.

Maps of Area: Trails Illustrated® – Steamboat Springs South / Routt National Forest

Rabbit Ears Peaks

Description of Trail: Start at the Continental Divide stone monument. Head North following the 2-track FR 311. The gate is often closed (until mid-summer) to motor vehicles because of late snow melt. On the right, in about 1/4 mile is FR 291. Follow this 2-track all the way to the base of the Rabbit Ears Peaks. There are 2 minor stream crossings and a few steeper grades. The final 100 yard ascent to the actual base of the Rabbit Ears is extremely steep and not suitable for the casual rider. Plan on walking up the final distance. The return ride is along the same route.

Map:

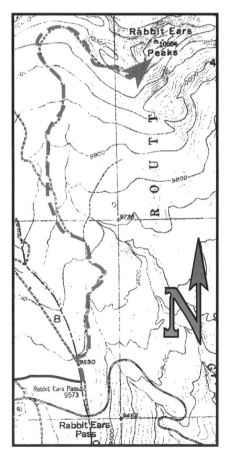

South Elk River Loop

Rated:

Location: North of Steamboat Springs; East of Clark; Seedhouse Road

Length: Trail length: 5 miles / Forest Road return: 7 miles / Total loop: 12 miles

Elevation: 7800′ to 8400′

Difficulty: Moderate efforts on the single track section, and 1 major stream crossing.

Highlights: Beautiful backcountry route. Elk are often seen in this area.

Directions to Trailhead: Head West out of Steamboat Springs to CO 129. Turn right toward Steamboat Lake and Clark. Just North of Clark is Seedhouse Road / FR 400. Head East on Seedhouse Road 6 miles to FR 441 turn right and look for the Hinman Day Use Parking Area just across the Elk River bridge.

Support and Facilities: Toilets are available at the Hinman Campground. Fuel, food, and restaurant available in Clark.

Maps of Area: Trails Illustrated® – Steamboat Springs North & Hahn's Peak / Routt National Forest

South Elk River Loop

Description of Trail: Description of Trail: The single track TR 1100A starts at the head of the parking lot. The trail draws closer to the South Branch of the Elk River until it reaches a crossing. This can be quite tricky in the Springtime high water. At any time, it is cold and rocky. After the crossing, continue through varying habitats along the course of the river valley. TR 1100 intersects at about the half way point. The bike route continues on TR 1100 until it ends at FR 402. Turn left and enjoy the descent to Seedhouse Road. Turn left again to complete the loop. It is suggested to travel the loop in this direction to take advantage of the downhill grade on Seedhouse Road.

Map:

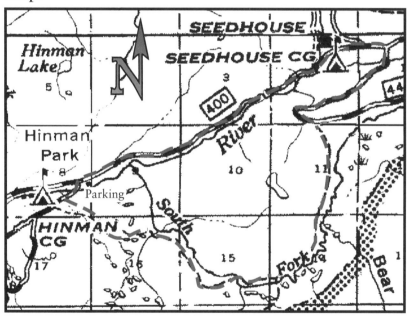

Spring Creek Park

Rated:

Location: North side of Steamboat Springs

Length: Easy route: 4 miles round trip Long loop route: *Not determined yet.* *Note: Still being planned for final placement of second trailhead off Buffalo Pass Road (across from Dry Lake Campground).

Elevation: Easy route (A): 6800´ to 7000´ Long loop route(B): 6800´ to 8300´

Difficulty: Route A: easy family level ride.
Route B: Vigorous effort and skills required.

Highlights: Spring Creek Park is a lovely area newly developed. The lower trail follows a very pleasant stream valley. The upper section is a fun ride.

Directions to Trailhead: In Steamboat Springs, turn North on 3rd Street. This is the road to Fish Creek Falls. It jogs right then heads uphill. Turn left after just over 100 yards on Amethyst Drive. In about 1/4 mile look for Spring Creek access road on the right. Parking is suggested at the beginning of this access road. Second trailhead: Follow Strawberry Park Road to Buffalo Pass Road. Turn right, and continue to Dry Lake Campground's Staging (Parking) Area.

Support and Facilities: Spring Creek Mountain Park has toilets, picnic sites, and water available. Fuel and food supplies available in Steamboat Springs.

Maps of Area: Trails Illustrated® – Clark, Buffalo Pass & Steamboat Springs North & South / Routt National Forest

Spring Creek Park

Description of Trail: Route A (easy): Start at parking area following the road until it comes to the main park area. Bear left on the 2-track road heading around and above the ponds. The trail will follow the course of Spring Creek for about 2 miles from the trail head. Turn around at the bridge crossing the creek. Route B* (hard): The trail is proposed to follow hill contours before it becomes a fun single track downhill to the finish. Some sections through private land. *Route B is not developed as of publishing date. Development scheduled for 1993. Please be aware of other trail users in the main park area.

Map:

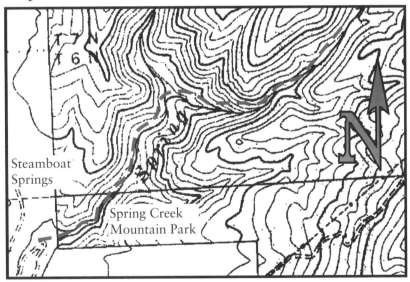

Tepee Creek Trail

Rated:

Location: Lynx Pass; Southeast of Stagecoach Lake State Park

Length: Trail: 4 miles Loop Return: 11 miles total

Elevation: 9000′ to 9300′

Difficulty: Moderate skills and water crossing abilities required.

Highlights: Very scenic single track trail. Low traffic road return loop. Lots of beaver activity.

Directions to Trailhead: Take US 40 South from Steamboat Springs 3 miles to CO 131. Turn right and travel to Co. 16 toward Stagecoach Lake. On the South side of the lake is Co. 16/FR 270. Turn left (East) on this paved road. It later turns to gravel but continues to the Lynx Pass Campground. FR 263 is 1/4 mile past the campground. Turn left on FR 263 for 1/2 mile. Parking is on the road. An alternate route is CO 131 to Toponas, left on CO 134 to Lynx Pass Road (FR 270).

Support and Facilities: Toilets and water are available at the Lynx Pass Campground. Fuel and food are available in Oak Creek and Toponas.

Maps of Area: Trails Illustrated® – Yampa, Gore Pass/ Routt National Forest

Tepee Creek Trail

Description of Trail: From FR 263 the trail immediately turns right after a small creek crossing. The first mile climbs through a delightful forest, then crosses FR 263 and continues as a brief 2-track. It quickly narrows back to single track. The trail occasionally becomes flooded due to beaver activity so some creative riding may be necessary to stay dry. The trail follows the North side of this creek valley. Cross an old logging road and continue on the trail until Tepee Creek joins Rock Creek. Cross Rock Creek, turn right for the short .2 miles to FR 250. Follow FR 250 to CO 134. Turn right toward FR 270 (Lynx Pass Road) with another right turn to complete the loop.

Map:

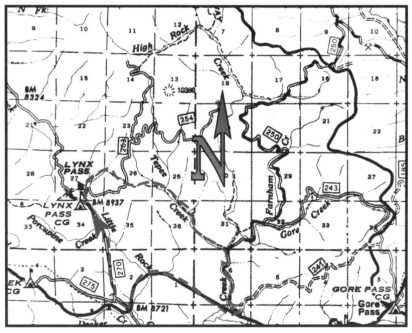

The Divide Trail

Rated:

Location: Rabbit Ears Pass; Buffalo Pass

Length: 14 miles one way

Elevation: Rabbit Ears staging area: 9600´ Buffalo Pass staging area: 10,300´

Difficulty: Rugged single track sections. Its length and altitude make this ride not for inexperienced riders. Round trips difficult.

Highlights: A excellent high country ride along the Continental Divide. Many lakes, streams, and high meadows along the route. Views, vistas, and animals.

Directions to Trailhead: Rabbit Ears Pass: Take US 40 South from Steamboat Springs. On the left is the Dumont Lake turn off about 18 miles from town. Park in the Day Use Area or by the rock monument. Buffalo Pass*: Head North out of Steamboat Springs on 7th Street toward Strawberry Park. Buffalo Pass Road / Co 60 is on the right. Head up this Forest Road for the 11 miles required to reach the summit. *Difficult for passenger vehicles.

Support and Facilities: Toilets and water available at Dumont Lake. Toilets at Summit Lake Campground. Fuel and food supplies in Steamboat Springs.

Maps of Area: Trails Illustrated® – Steamboat Springs South / Routt National Forest

The Divide Trail

Description of Trail: May be started at either trailhead. Suggested start is from Rabbit Ears Pass. Follow the 2-track FR 311 for approximately 4 miles to TR 1101 on the right. This single track provides many challenges from steep descents, minor stream crossings, to rocky ascents. Continue past the 4-way intersection with TR 1134 / TR1102. This last section intersects FR 310. Turn right to head for Buffalo Pass. Side trips to Percy and Round Lake on TR 1134. Side trip to Long Lake on TR 1102. It is *not recommended* to return to Steamboat Springs via TR 1102 in Fish Creek Canyon. It is very technical and usually crowded with hikers.

Map:

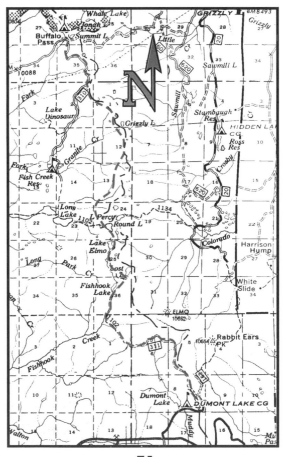

Walton Peak

Rated:

Location: Rabbit Ears Pass; South of Steamboat Springs

Length: 5.5 miles one way

Elevation: 9500′ to 10,500′

Difficulty: Moderate initial climb, then rolling. Final ascent is very strenuous.

Highlights: Excellent views along the route and at the "near" summit of Walton Peak.

Directions to Trailhead: Head South out of Steamboat Springs on US 40. Continue towards Rabbit Ears Pass to the Dumont Lake turnoff approximately 18 miles. Opposite this turnoff, on the right is FR 251. Park here or at the staging lot on US 40.

Support and Facilities: Toilets, water, and picnic sites available at Dumont Lake Day Use Area. Fuel and food available in Steamboat Springs.

Maps of Area: Trails Illustrated® – Steamboat Springs South / Routt National Forest

Walton Peak

Description of Trail: This is a 2-track jeep trail all the way to Walton Peak. Start by climbing 3 miles on FR 251. There is a nice lookout on the left at about 2 miles along the way. Turn right at the first trail intersection. This will still be FR 251. The 2-track now follows an open stream valley with meadows, ponds, and potential wildlife viewing for the next 2 miles to the base of Walton Peak. It is only 1/2 mile to the top from this point but is fairly steep. The actual top is heavily forested without any open views but 100 yards short of the very end is a wonderful lookout. This is an ideal destination for a rest or picnic. Return the same route.

Map:

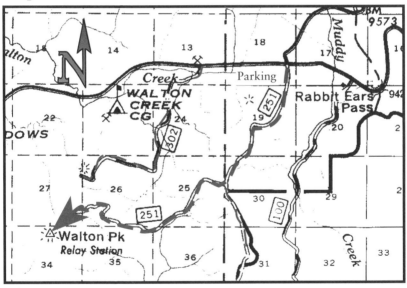

West Gore Pass

Rated:

Location: Gore Pass; East of Toponas; Southwest of Kremmling

Length: Loop routes of 10, 17, 27, 27.5 miles

Elevation: Varies per route: 8800′ to 10,000′ Gore Pass staging area: 9500′

Difficulty: Longer routes require climbing long grades. Bobcat Trail (FR 185) has steep descent sections. Light traffic on paved CO 134.

Highlights: Great backcountry routes not requiring technical skills. Especially good for group tours.

Directions to Trailhead: Head South from Steamboat Springs on US 40. Turn right on CO 131 toward Oak Creek. Continue past Oak Creek on CO 131 to Toponas. Turn left on CO 134. Travel past Lynx Pass turn off for another 6.5 miles. Look for FR 243 on the left opposite Gore Pass Campground. Park at the Day Use lot at Gore Pass.

Support and Facilities: Toilets available at Gore Pass Campground. Fuel and food available in Toponas. Restaurants available in Yampa and Oak Creek.

Maps of Area: Trails Illustrated® – Yampa, Gore Pass / Routt National Forest

West Gore Pass

Description of Trail: All loops are on Forest Roads, some with a brief paved road connection.

Loop A: FR 243 - left on FR 241 - left on CO 134- return. (10 mi.)

Loop B: FR 243 - left on FR 250 - left on CO 134 - return. (17 mi.)

Loop C: FR 243- right on FR 185 - left on FR 100 - left on FR 250 - left on FR 243 - return. (27 mi.)

Loop D: FR 243 - right on FR 185 - left on FR 100 - left on FR 250 - left on CO 134 - return. (27.5 mi.)

Map:

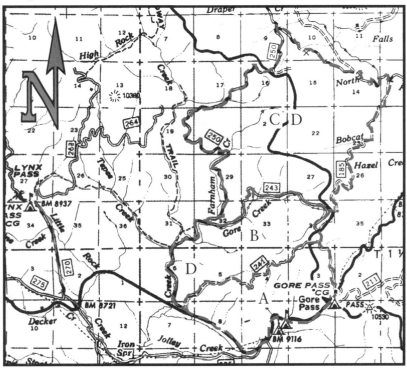

International Mountain Bicycling Association
IMBA RULES OF THE TRAIL©

1. **Ride on open trails only.** Respect trail and road closures (ask if not sure), avoid possible trespass on private land, obtain permits and authorization as may be required. Federal and State wilderness areas are closed to cycling.

2. **Leave no trace.** Be sensitive to the dirt beneath you. Even on open trails, you should not ride under conditions where you will leave evidence of your passing, such as on certain soils shortly after a rain. Observe the different types of soils and trail construction; practice low-impact cycling. This also means staying on the trail and not creating any new ones. Be sure to pack out at least as much as you pack in.

3. **Control your bicycle!** Inattention for even a second can cause disaster. Excessive speed maims and threatens people; there is no excuse for it!

4. **Always yield the trail.** Make your approach known well in advance with a friendly greeting (or a bell) is considerate and works well; starling someone may cause loss of trail access. Show your respect when passing others by slowing to a walk or even stopping. Anticipate that other trail users may be around corners or in blind spots.

5. **Never spook animals.** All animals are startled by an unannounced approach, a sudden movement, or a loud noise. This can be dangerous for you, for others, and for the animals. Give animal extra room and time to adjust to you. In passing, use special care and follow the directions of horseback riders (ask if uncertain). Running cattle and disturbing wild animals is a serious offense. Leave gates as you found them, or as marked.

6. Plan ahead. Know your equipment, your ability, and the area in which you are riding - and prepare accordingly. Be self-sufficient at all times. Wear a helmet, keep your machine in good condition, and carry necessary supplies for changes in weather or other conditions. A well-executed trip is a satisfaction to you and not a burden or offense to others.©

Courtesy of the INTERNATIONAL MOUNTAIN BIKE ASSOCIATION (IMBA)

The Muddy Slide, south of Stagecoach Lake, is a facinating place along the Morrison Divide Trail.

TIPS, TRAPS, & TALES

1. TIP: Use an extra waterbottle for tool storage if there is no other place available.

2. TRAP: Letting your back tire skid while braking as it will rarely go where you want and messes up the trail.

3. TIP: Small close fitting backpacks that x/c skiers use work well while biking.

4. TRAP: Going too far if you are not used to altitude. If you are new to biking the area plan on half your normal distance for the trip or Search and Rescue may have to help you out with the other half.

5. TRAP: Thinking water is still pure in the mountains and doesn't need treatment before drinking.

6. TRAP: Disregarding the above.

7. TIP: A shower cap makes a great rain cover over a helmet.

8. TRAP: Riding without wearing bright orange clothes during hunting season.

9. TIP: There are local hot spring pools for relaxing after a day on the bike.

10. TIP: Freeze a carton of your favorite fruit juice and you will find a great cool drink waiting for you later on.

11. TIP: Bananas really are a bicyclists' favorite food. They even come wrapped!

12. TRAP: Assuming the weather will be stable all day in the mountains. It is very changeable and it can snow any day of the year.

13. Trap: Thinking the little black and white striped kitty along the trail is just a little kitty.

14. TIP: Look where you want to go while riding. This seems simple but by concentrating on the best route through or around a bad section you will find yourself much more likely to go through cleanly.

15. TIP: Watch your tire inflation pressure. Tires expand at altitude and compress on the decent.

16. TIP: Use the widest gear combination you can fit on you bike. Granny gears, aka ..whimpy gears, can get you to the top with less effort. "Its not how fast you get there its just getting there that counts."..The Author

17. TRAP: Getting a bike with too large of a frame. The gearing doesn't change with the size of the bike, just the geometry for clearance and safety.

18. TALES: Some MTB bikers are taking cellular phones with them in case of emergency. Its true!!

19. TIP: The use of special RV toilet paper can lessen the impact in the backcountry when buried properly.

20. TIP: A seal-a-meal bag will protect and store tubes and tools. Seal in a baby powdered tire tube for future use. It will keep clean and dry and ready for use .

21. TRAP: No pre-planning can mean no return.

22. TIP: Wear calf high socks in the back country. The ankle part can be used to dry wet feet after barefoot stream crossings. They also protect the shins from pedal strikes when walking the bike on narrow sections.

23. TIP: Climbing is more efficient by pulling straight back, not up, on the handlebars.

24. TALE: Electric powered bicycles are now available. Soon to come with solar power!

BIBLIOGRAPHY

SELECTIVE READING LIST

THE COMPLETE MOUNTAIN BIKER,
Dennis Coello

MOUNTAIN BIKING SKILLS, Editors of
Bicycling Magazine

600 TIPS FOR BETTER BICYCLING, Editors
of Bicycling Magazine

MEDICINE FOR THE BACKCOUNTRY,
Buck Tilton and Frank Hubbell

HIKING THE 'BOAT, Diane White-Crane

ORGANIZATIONS

IMBA - INTERNATIONAL MOUNTAIN
BIKE ASSOCIATION
P.O. Box 412053
Los Angeles, CA 90041
(818) 796-1283

ROUTT COUNTY RIDERS
P.O. Box 770094
Steamboat Springs CO 80477

NORBA - NATIONAL OFF-ROAD BICYCLE ASSOCIATION

P.O. Box 1901
Chandler, AZ 85244
(602) 961-0635

INDEX

Index continued:

FIELD NOTES